CHERISH THE CAT

CHERISH THE CAT

Edited by
Jane Parker Resnick

Longmeadow Press

Cover design by Kelvin P. Oden

Interior design by Allan Mogel

ISBN: 0-681-417374

Printed in United States of America

First Edition

0 9 8 7 6 5 4 3 2 1

Contents

HEARTH

A cat sat quaintly by the fire
   And watched the burning coals
And watched the little flames aspire
   Like small decrepit souls.
Queer little fire with coals so fat
   And crooked flames that rise,
No queerer than the little cat.
   With fire in its eyes.

Peggy Bacon

I had only one cat, and he was more a companion than a cat. When he departed this life I did not care to, as many men do when their partners die, take a second.

Charles Dudley Warner

Cats are a mysterious kind of folk.
There is more passing in their minds than we are aware of.
Sir Walter Scott

THE CAT BY THE FIRE

Poor Pussy! she looks up at us again, as if she thanked us for those vindications of dinner; and symbolically gives a twist of a yawn and a lick of her whiskers. Now she proceeds to clean herself all over, having a just sense of the demands of her elegant person— beginning judiciously with her paws, and fetching amazing tongues at her hind-hips. Anon, she scratches her neck with a foot of rapid delight, leaning her head towards it, and shutting her eyes, half to accommodate the action of the skin, and half to enjoy the luxury. She then rewards her paws with a few more touches; look at the action of her head and neck, how pleasing it is, the ears pointed forward, and the neck gently arching to and fro. Finally, she gives a sneeze, and another twist of mouth and whiskers, and then, curling her tail towards her front claws, settles herself on her hind quarters, in an attitude of bland meditation . . .

Leigh Hunt

THE WELL-BEHAVED CAT
GRISETTE DINES

Always well behaved am I,
Never scratch and never cry;
Only touch the diner's hand,
So that he can understand
That I want a modest share
Of the good things that are there.
If he pay but scanty heed
To my little stomach's need,
I beg him with a mew polite
To give me just a single bite.
Greedy though that diner be,
He will share his meal with me.

by Antoinette Deshoulières

To gain the friendship of a cat is a difficult thing. The cat is a philosophical, methodical, quiet animal, tenacious of its own habits, fond of order and cleanliness, and does not lightly confer its friendship, If you are worthy of its affection, a cat will be your friend but never your slave. He keeps his free will, though he loves, and he will not do for you what he thinks is unreasonable; but once he gives himself to you, it is with such absolute confidence, such fidelity of affection.

Theophile Gautier

THE KITTEN AND THE
FALLING LEAVES

That way look, my Infant, lo!
What a pretty baby-show!
See the Kitten on the wall,
Sporting with the leaves that fall,
Withered leaves—one—two—and three—
From the lofty elder-tree!
Through the calm and frosty air
Of this morning bright and fair,
Eddying round and round they sink
Softly, slowly: one might think,
From the motions that are made,
Every little leaf conveyed
Sylph or Fairy hither tending—
To this lower world descending,
Each invisible and mute,
In his wavering parachute.
But the Kitten, how she starts,
Crouches, stretches, paws, and darts!
First at one, and then its fellow
Just as light and just as yellow;
There are many now—now one—
Now they stop and there are none.
What intenseness of desire
In her upward eye of fire!
With a tiger-leap half-way
Now she meets the coming prey,

Lets it go as fast, and then
Has it in her power again:
Now she works with three or four,
Like an Indian conjuror;
Quick as he in feats of art,
Far beyond in joy of heart.

Were her antics played in the eye
Of a thousand standers-by,
Clapping hands with shout and stare,
What would little Tabby care
For the plaudits of the crowd?
Over happy to be proud,
Over wealthy in the treasure
Of her own exceeding pleasure!

William Wordsworth

GRAY THRUMS

Which is the cosiest voice,
The piping droning noise
    When the kettle hums,
Or this little old-fashioned wheel
    Spinning gray thrums?

Gray thrums! what wheel, you ask,
Turns as such pleasant task
    With a soft whirr?
Why, the one in pussy's throat
    That makes her purr.

Listen the rippling sound,
And think how round and round
    The spindle goes,
As the drowsy thread she spins
    Drowsily grows.

What will she do with it
When it is finished?   Knit
    Some mittens new?
Or shuttle it, and weave cloth
    As weavers do?

A funny idea that,
A spinning wheel in a cat!
Yet how it hums!
Our puss is gray, so of course
She spins gray thrums.

Clara Doty Bates

A dog is okay
On a sunny day
But a cat
Is where it's at.
Paula Scher

THE WHITE CAT AND THE STUDENT

I and Pangur Bán, my cat,
'Tis a like task we are at;
Hunting mice is his delight,
Hunting words I sit all night.

—*Anonymous*

It is a very inconvenient habit of kittens
(Alice had once made the remark) that,
whatever you say to them they always purr.
Lewis Carroll

TO A CAT

Cat! who has pass'd thy grand climacteric,
How many mice and rats hast in thy days
Destroy'd?—How many titbits stolen? Gaze
With those bright languid segments green, and prick
Those velvet ears—but prithee do not stick
Thy latent talons in me—and upraise
Thy gentle mew—and tell me all thy frays
Of fish and mice, and rats and tender chick.
Nay, look not down, nor lick thy dainty wrists—
For all the wheezy asthma—and for all
Thy tail's tip is nick'd off—and though the fists
Of many a maid have given thee many a maul,
Still is that fur as soft as when the lists
In youth thou enter'dst on glass-bottled wall.

John Keats

A kitten is in the animal world what a rosebud is in a garden.
Robert Southey

JUBILATE AGNO

For I will consider my Cat Jeoffrey

For he is the servant of the Living God, duly and daily serving him.

For at the First glance of the glory of God in the East he worships in his way.

For having done duty and received blessing he begins to consider himself.

For having consider'd God and himself he will consider his neighbor.

For if he meets another cat he will kiss her in kindness.

For when he takes his prey he plays with it to give it a chance.

For he keeps the Lord's watch in the night against the adversary.

For he counteracts the powers of darkness by his electrical skin & glaring eyes.

For he purrs in thankfulness, when God tells him he's a good Cat.

For he is an instrument for the children to learn benevolence upon.

For there is nothing sweeter than his peace when at rest.

For there is nothing brisker than his life in motion.
For God has blessed him in the variety of his
movements.
For every house is incomplete without him and a
blessing is lacking in the spirit.

Christopher Smart

God gave man the cat in order that he might have the pleasure of caressing
the tiger.

Proverb

KITTEN'S NIGHT THOUGHTS

When Human Folk put out the light
And think they've made it dark as night,
A Pussycat sees every bit
As well as when the lights are lit.

When Human Folk have gone upstairs
And shed their skins and said their prayers,
And there is no one to annoy,
Then Pussy may her life enjoy.

No human hands to pinch or slap,
Or rub her fur against the nap,
Or throw cold water from a pail,
Or make a handle of her tail.

And so you will not think it wrong,
When she can play the whole night long,
With no one to disturb her play,
That Pussy goes to bed by day.

Oliver Herford

The cat, which is a solitary beast, is single minded and goes its way alone, but the dog, like his master, is confused in his mind.

H.G. Wells

CATMINT

Bear in mind
   Never to push a cat from behind;
   There is no humiliation for a cat
   Greater than that.

   Cats are proud
And no familiarity is allowed.
   To a friend
They will condescend
And occasionally are seen
   To lean;
But they will not go out of their way
   To betray
Signs of affection
Or recollection
Nor will incline their ears
   To taunts or jeers.
At the least presentiment
   Of sentiment
They simply retire
   In ire.
Do not shout or call
That will not do at all.
Fish and milk
   And that ilk

May be used as easement
   And appeasement
But even mice
Do not entice
   The well-bred,
For the cat
   Is an aristocrat;
Get that into your head.

Eric Clough Taylor

No. Heaven will not ever Heaven be
Unless my cats are there to welcome me.
Anonymous

THE KITTEN SPEAKS

I am the Cat of Cats. I am
    The everlasting cat!
Cunning, and old, and sleek as jam,
    The everlasting cat!
I hunt the vermin in the night—
    The everlasting cat!
For I see best without the light—
    The everlasting cat!

William Brighty Rands

*If animals could speak as fabulists have feigned, . . . the cat would have
the rare talent of never saying a word too much.*

P.G. Hamerton

CATS

A dog will often steal a bone,
But conscience lets him not alone,
And by his tail his guilt is known.

But cats consider theft a game,
And, howsoever you may blame,
Refuse the slightest sign of shame.

Anonymous

Cat. n. A soft, indestructible automaton provided by nature to be kicked when things go wrong in the domestic circle.

Ambrose Bierce

CATS

On the last Mayday morning my cat brought
Into the world six darling little kittens,
May-kittens, all pure white with black tail-tippings.
Indeed, it was a decorative childbed.
The cook, however—cooks are savage beings,
And human kindness grows not in a kitchen—
Five of the six she meant to take and drown them,
Five white, but tipped-with-black-tail, Mayday kittens
This monstrous woman had marked down to kill.
I took her down a peg. May heaven bless
Me for my human feeling! The dear kittens,
They grew and grew, and in a short while ventured
With high tails walking over court and hearth;
Yes, as the cook sadistically noticed,
They grew and grew, and nightly at her window
They practised out their darling little voices.
I, for my part, as I now saw them growing,
I prized myself and my humanity.

A year is round, and they are cats, those kittens,
And it is Mayday! How can I describe it,
The scene that now enacts itself before me?
My whole house, from the cellar to the gable,
Its every single corner is a childbed!
Here one is lying, there another kitten,
In cupboards, baskets, under stairs and table;

The old cat even—no, I dare not say it,
Lies in the cook's own maiden-modest bed.
And each, yes, each one of the seven she-cats,
Has seven, think, has seven youthful kittens,
May-kittens, all pure white with black tail-tippings.
The cook is raving. I can set no bounds
To the blind anger of this dreadful female.
She will go out and drown all nine-and forty!
Yet I myself, my head recoils from it:
O human kindness, how can I preserve you?
What can I do with six-and-fifty cats?

Theodor Storm

If man could be crossed with the cat,
it would improve man but deteriorate the cat.
Mark Twain

TO A CAT

I

Stately, lordly friend,
    Condescend
Here to sit by me, and turn
Glorious eyes that smile and burn,
Golden eyes, love's lustrous meed,
On the golden page I read.

All your wondrous wealth of hair,
    Dark and fair,
Silken-shaggy, soft and bright
As the clouds and beams of night,
Pays my reverent hand's caress
Back with friendlier gentleness.

Dogs may fawn on all and some
    As they come;
You, a friend of loftier mind,
Answer friends alone in kind.
Just your foot upon my hand
Softly bids it understand.

Algernon Charles Swinburne

There is no kitten too little to scratch.
Proverb

ODE ON THE DEATH OF A FAVORITE CAT, DROWNED IN A TUB OF GOLD FISHES

'Twas on a lofty vase's side,
Where China's gayest art had dy'd
    The azure flowers that blow;
Demurest of the tabby kind,
The pensive Selima reclin'd,
    Gazed on the lake below.

Her conscious tail her joy declar'd;
The fair round face, the snowy beard,
    The velvet of her paws,
Her coat, that with the tortoise vies,
Her ears of jet, and emerald eyes,
    She saw; and purr'd applause.

Still had she gaz'd; but 'midst the tide
Two angel forms were seen to glide,
    The Genii of the stream:
Their scaly armour's Tyrian hue
Thro' richest purple to the view
    Betray'd a golden gleam.

The hapless Nymph with wonder saw:
A whisker first and then a claw,
   With many an ardent wish,
She stretch'd in vain to reach the prize,
What female heart can gold despise?
   What Cat's averse to fish?
Presumptuous Maid! with looks intent
Again she stretch'd, again she bent,
   Nor knew the gulf between.
(Malignant Fate sat by, and smil'd)
The slipp'ry verge her feet beguil'd.
   She tumbled headlong in.

Eight times emerging from the flood.
She mew'd to ev're watry God,
   Some speedy aid to send.
No Dolphin came, no Nereid stirr'd:
Nor cruel *Tom*, nor *Susan* heard.
   A Fav'rite has no friend!

From hence, ye Beauties, undeceiv'd,
Know, one false step is ne'er retriev'd,
   And be with caution bold.
Not all that tempts your wand'ring eyes
And heedless hearts, is lawful prize;
   Nor all that glisters, gold.

Thomas Gray

No matter how much cats fight, there always seem to be plenty of kittens.
Abraham Lincoln

Cats are rather delicate creatures and they are subject to a good many different ailments, but I never heard of one who suffered from insomnia.

Joseph Wood Krutch

TO A CAT

There is no reason I can find
That you should make me feel so small;
I have a fair to middling mind
While you have almost none at all.
No proud position do you fill;
Your features are extremely plain
And yet I wilt beneath your chill
Disdain.

At night I lie back in my chair
From all my work and worry free
And then I see that sneering stare
Which, from the hearth, you fix on me.
I know I should not strive to please
A dull, unprepossessing cat
But I'm distrait and ill at ease
At that.

You have no power to decide
What I have done or left undone,
You're totally unqualified
For criticising anyone.

Anonymous

All cats and kittens, whether royal Persians or of the lowliest estate, resent patronage, jocoseness (which they rightly hold to be in bad taste), and demonstrative affection—those lavish embraces which lack delicacy and reserve.

Agnes Repplier

THE WILLOW CATS

They call them pussy-willows,
  But there's no cat to see
Except the little furry toes
  That stick out on the tree:

I think that very long ago,
  When I was just born new,
There must have been whole pussy-cats
  Where just the toes stick through—

And every Spring it worries me,
  I cannot ever find
Those willow-cats that ran away
  And left their toes behind!

Margaret Widdemer

TWO LITTLE KITTENS

Two little kittens, one stormy night,
Began to quarrel, and then to fight;
One had a mouse, the other had none,
And that's the way the quarrel begun.

"I'll have that mouse," said the biggest cat;
"You'll have that mouse? We'll see about that!"
"I *will* have that mouse," said the eldest son;
"You *shan't* have the mouse," said the little one.

I told you before 'twas a stormy night
When these two little kittens began to fight;
The old woman seized her sweeping broom,
And swept the two kittens right out of the room.

The ground was covered with frost and snow,
And the two little kittens had nowhere to go;
So they laid them down on the mat at the door,
While the old woman finished sweeping the floor.

Then they crept in, as quiet as mice,
All wet with the snow, and as cold as ice,
For they found it was better, that stormy night,
To lie down and sleep than to quarrel and fight.

Anonymous

In a cat's eyes all things belong to cats.
English saying

THE LITTLE CAT ANGEL

The ghost of a little white kitten
Crying mournfully, early and late,
Distracted St. Peter, the watchman,
As he guarded the heavenly gate.
"Say, what do you mean," said his saintship,
"Coming here and behaving like that?"
I want to see Nellie, my missus,"
Sobbed the wee little ghost of a cat.
"I know she's not happy without me,
Won't you open and let me go in?"
"Begone," gasped the horrified watchman,
"Why the very idea is a sin;
I open the gate to good angels,
Not to stray little beggars like you."
"All right," mewed the little white kitten,
"Though a cat I'm a good angel, too."
Amazed at so bold an assertion,
But aware that he must make no mistake,
In silence, St. Peter long pondered,
For his name and repute were at stake,
Then placing the cat in his bosom
With a "Whist now, and say all your prayers,"
He opened the heavenly portals
And ascended the bright golden stairs.
A little girl angel came flying,
"That's my kitty, St. Peter," she cried.

And, seeing the joy of their meeting,
Peter let the cat angel abide.

This tale is the tale of a kitten
Dwelling now with the blessed above,
It vanquished grim Death and High Heaven
For the name of the kitten was Love.

Leontine Stanfield

An overdressed woman is like a cat dressed in saffron.
Egyptian proverb

THE TYGER

Tyger! Tyger! burning bright
In the forests of the night,
What immortal hand or eye
Could frame thy fearful symmetry?

In what distant deeps or skies
Burnt the fire of thine eyes?
On what wings dare he aspire?
What the hand dare seize the fire?

And what shoulder, & what art,
Could twist the sinews of thy heart?
And when thy heart began to beat,
What dread hand? & what dread feet?

What the hammer? what the chain?
In what furnace was thy brain?
What the anvil? what dread grasp
Dare its deadly terrors clasp?

When the stars threw down their spears,
And water'd heaven with their tears,
Did he smile his work to see?
Did he who made the Lamb make thee?

Tyger! Tyger! burning bright
In the forests of the night,
What immortal hand or eye,
Dare frame thy fearful symmetry?

William Blake

Cats are admirable company. I am very fond of dogs, too; but their sphere is the field. In the house they do not understand that repose of manner which is the soul of breeding. The cat's manners or rather manner seems to have been perfected by generations, nay centuries, of familiar intercourse with the great and cultivated of the earth.

Algernon S. Logan

The smallest feline is a masterpiece.
Leonardo Da Vinci

THE OWL AND THE PUSSY-CAT

I

The Owl and the Pussy-cat went to sea
    In a beautiful pea-green boat,
They took some honey, and plenty of money,
    Wrapped up in a five-pound note.
The Owl looked up to the stars above,
    And sang to a small guitar,
'O lovely Pussy! O Pussy, my love,
    What a beautiful Pussy you are,
        You are,
        You are!
    What a beautiful Pussy you are!'
And hand in hand, on the edge of the sand,
    They danced by the light of the moon,
        The moon,
        The moon,
They danced by the light of the moon.

II

Pussy said to the Owl, 'You elegant fowl!
    How charmingly sweet you sing!
O let us be married! too long we have tarried:
    But what shall we do for a ring?'
They sailed away, for a year and a day,
    To the land where the Bong-tree grows

And there in a wood a Piggy-wig stood
  With a ring at the end of his nose,
        His nose,
        His nose,
With a ring at the end of his nose.

III

'Dear Pig, are you willing to sell for one shilling
  Your ring?' Said the Piggy, 'I will.'
So they took it away, and were married next day
  By the Turkey who lives on the hill.
They dined on mince, and slices of quince.
  Which they ate with a runcible spoon;
And hand in hand, on the edge of the sand,
  They danced by the light of the moon,
        The moon,
        The moon,
They danced by the light of the moon.

Edward Lear

(The cat is) . . . *the only non-gregarious domestic animal. it is retained by its extraordinary adhesion to the comforts of the house in which it is reared.*

Francis Galton

UNDER-THE-TABLE MANNERS

It's very hard to be polite
   If you're a cat.
When other folks are up at table
Eating all that they are able,
   You are down upon the mat
   If you're a cat.

You're expected just to sit
   If you're a cat.
Not to let them know you're there
By scratching at the chair,
   Or a light, respected pat
   If you're a cat.

You are not to make a fuss
   If you're a cat.
Tho' there's fish upon the plate
You're expected just to wait,
   Wait politely on the mat
   If you're a cat.

Anonymous

(The cat is) . . . *an example of sophistication minus civilization.*
Anon.

NIGHT

The night is coming softly, slowly;
Look, it's getting hard to see.
    Through the windows,
    Through the door,
    Pussyfooting
    On the floor,
    Dragging shadows,
    Crawling,
    Creeping,
    Soon it will be time for sleeping.
Pull down the shades.
Turn on the light.
Let's pretend it isn't night.

Mary Ann Hoberman

The Cat always leaves her mark upon her friends.
Spanish Saying

THE STRAY

The Cat, who sleeps upon the mat,
  Is not domestic as she seems:
From Amazon to Ararat,
  She prowls in her majestic dreams.
Each Alley Cat has power to stray
  In sleep, from dusty afternoon,
To pad along the Milky Way,
  and tip the saucer of the moon.

And, whosoever killed the Cat,
  Was not dull Care, as some declare—
She roams—the world's Immortal Stray—
  From Babylon to Finisterre.
And when, in sunny sitting-room,
  We see her sleep, with paws a-twitch,
She's clinging to a flying broom
  Behind a sleeping witch.

Barbara Euphan Todd

We tie bright ribbons around their necks, and occasionally little tinkling bells and we affect to think that they are as sweet and vapid as the coy name "kitty" by which we call them would imply. It is a curious illusion. for, purring beside our fireplaces and pattering along our back fences, we have go a wild beast as uncowed and uncorrupted as nay under heaven.

Alan Devoe
Plain and Fancy Cats

ON A CAT AGEING

He blinks upon the hearth-rug
And yawns in deep content,
Accepting all the comforts
That Providence has sent.

Louder he purrs, and louder,
In one glad hymn of praise,
For all the night's adventures,
For quiet, restful days.

Life will go on for ever,
With all that cat can wish;
Warmth, and the glad procession
Of fish, and milk and fish.

Only—the thought disturbs him—
He's noticed once or twice,
The times are somehow breeding
A nimbler race of mice.

Alexander Gray

I saw the most beautiful cat today. It was sitting by the side of the road, its two front feet neatly and graciously together. Then it gravely swished around its tail to completely and snugly encircle itself. It was so fit *and beautifully neat, that gesture, and so self-satisfied—so complacent.*

Anne Morrow Lindbergh,
Bring Me a Unicorn

MONTAGUE MICHAEL

Montague Michael
You're much too fat,
You wicked old, wily old,
Well-fed cat.

All night you sleep
On a cushion of silk,
And twice a day
I bring you milk.

And once in a while,
When you catch a mouse,
You're the proudest person
In all the house.

Anonymous

I have noticed that what cats most appreciate in a human being is not the ability to produce food which they take for granted—but his or her entertainment value.

Geoffrey Household

THE CATS OF KILKENNY

There were once two cats of Kilkenny,
Each thought there was one cat too many;
So they fought and they fit,
And they scratched and they bit,
Till, excepting their nails
And the tips of their tails,
Instead of two cats, there weren't any.

Anonymous

No favor can win gratitude from a cat.
La Fontaine

A kitten is so flexible that she is almost double; the hind parts are equivalent to another kitten with which the forepart plays. She does not discover that her tail belongs to her until you tread upon it.

Henry David Thoreau

MARIGOLD

She moved through the garden in glory, because
She had very long claws at the end of her paws.
Her back was arched, her tail was high,
A green fire glared in her vivid eye;
And all the Toms, though never so bold,
Quailed at the martial Marigold.

Richard Garnett

When I play with my cat, who knows whether she is not amusing herself with me more than I with her.

Montaigne

Cats know how to obtain food without labor, shelter without confinement, and love without penalities.

W.L. George

CATS

Cats, no less liquid than their shadows,
Offer no angles to the wind.
They slip, diminished, neat, through loopholes
Less than themselves.

A.S.J. Tessimond

(The cat is) . . . a pygmy lion who loves mice, hates dogs, and patronizes human beings.

Oliver Herford

I have loved my cats with a curious kind of affection unlike that of any other emotion that I have experienced for man or beast . . . I think that it is compounded of admiration, sympathy, and amusement. To this I add a slight and curious tincture of pity plus a wholly unpredictable and irrational feeling which comes welling up out of depths indefinable.

Paul Gallico

THE GREATER CATS
WITH GOLDEN EYES

The greater cats with golden eyes
Stare out between the bars.
Deserts are there, and different skies,
And night with different stars.

Victoria Sackville-West

I think one reason we admire cats . . . is their proficiency in one-upmanship. They always seem to come out on top no matter what they are doing—or pretend they do. Rarely do you see a cat discomfited. They have no conscience, and they never regret. Maybe we secretly envy them.

Barbara Webster

He shut his eyes while Saha {the cat} kept vigil, watching all the invisible signs that hover over sleeping human beings when the light is put out.

Colette

Cats make exquisite photographs . . . They don't keep bouncing at you to be kissed just as you get the lens adjusted.

Gladys Taber

THE CAT OF THE HOUSE

Over the hearth with my 'minishing eyes I muse
Until after
The last coal dies.
Every tunnel of the mouse.
Every channel of the cricket.
I have smelt.
I have felt
The secret shifting of the mouldered rafter,
And heard
Every bird in the thicket.
I see
You
Nightingale up in your tree!
I, born of a race of strange things,
Of deserts, great temples, great kings,
In the hot sands where the nightingale never
      sings!

Ford Madox Ford

A dog is like a liberal. He wants to please everybody. A cat really doesn't need to know that everybody loves him.

William Kuntsler

THE RETIRED CAT

A Poet's cat, sedate and grave,
As poet well could wish to have,
Was much addicted to inquire
For nooks, to which she might retire,
And where, secure as mouse in chink,
She might repose, or sit and think.
I know not where she caught the trick—
Nature perhaps herself had cast her
In such a mould *philisophique,*
Or else she learned it of her master.

William Cowper

Purring would seem to be, in her case, an automatic safety-valve device for dealing with happiness overflow.

Monica Edwards

THAT CAT

The cat that comes to my window sill
When the moon looks cold and the night is still—
He comes in a frenzied state alone
With a tail that stands like a pine tree cone,
And says, "I have finished my evening lark,
And I think I can hear a hound dog bark.
My whiskers are frozen stuck to my chin.
I do wish you'd git up and let me in."
    That cat gits in.

But if in solitude of the night
He doesn't appear to be feeling right,
And rises and stretches and seeks the floor,
And some remote corner he would explore,
And doesn't feel satisfied just because
There's no good spot for to sharpen his claws,
And meows and canters uneasy about
Beyond the least shadow of any doubt
    That cat gits out.

Ben King

The cat is, above all things, a dramatist; its life is living in an endless romance.

Margaret Benson

MY CAT

Deep in my brain walks to and fro,
As well as in his own domain,
A handsome cat of gentle strain,—
Scarce can I hear his mew so low.

His tender call wakes not alarm,
But though he growl or softly sound,
Still is his voice rich and profound,—
There lies his secret and his charm.

No other bow can ever bring
From my heart's perfect instrument
Such royal notes of deep content
Or waken its most vibrant string.

Than can thy voice, mysterious Puss,
Scraphic cat, and cat most strange,
As a celestial, scorning change,
As subtle as harmonious.

With growing wonderment I see
The fire in thy pale pupils glow
Like watch lights when the sun is low,
Thy living opals gaze at me.

Charles Pierre Baudelaire

Everything that moves, serves to interest and amuse a cat. He is convinced that nature is busying herself with his diversion; he can conceive of no other purpose in the universe.

F.A. Paradis de Moncrif

THE LAZY PUSSY

There lives a good-for-nothing cat,
    So lazy it appears,
That chirping birds can safely come
    And light upon her ears.

And rats and mice can venture out
    To nibble at her toes,
Or climb around and pull her tail,
    And boldly scratch her nose.

Fine servants brush her silken coat
    And give her cream for tea;—
Yet she's a good-for-nothing cat,
    As all the world may see.

Palmer Cox

I love my cats because I enjoy my home; and little by little, they become its visible soul.

Jean Cocteau

Way down deep we're all motivated by the same urges. Cats have the courage to live by them.

Jim Davis

AT THE ZOO

In the great Zoological Gardens [of Marseille] we found specimens of all the animals the world produces, I think . . . The boon companion of the colossal elephant was a common cat! This cat had a fashion of climbing up the elephant's hind legs, and roosting on his back. She would sit up there, with her paws curved under her breast, and sleep in the sun half the afternoon. It used to annoy the elephant at first and he would reach up and take her down, but she would go aft and climb up again. She persisted until she finally conquered the elephant's prejudices, and now they are inseparable friends. The cat plays about her comrade's forefeet or his trunk often, until dogs approach, and then she goes aloft out of danger. The elephant has annihilated several dogs lately, that pressed his companion too closely.

Mark Twain

Balanchine has trained his cat to perform brilliant jetes *and* tours en l'air; *he says that at last he has a body worth choreographing for.*

Bernard Taper

THE WILD CAT

The wildcat sits on the rocks.
His hair is spitting fire
into the morning air.
His eyes are yellow.

Club-headed dynamic cat,
he is all power and force.
Among the dry green grass,
the hares are playing.

The air is clear and pure.
The hares are leaping and jumping
over invisible fences
of pure brilliant blue.

The wildcat sits by himself
on his stony throne, not thinking.
His fur simmers like fire
snarling and sparkling.

Iain Crichton Smith

The cat is the companion of the fireside.
Edward E. Whiting

THE LOVER WHOSE
MISTRESS FEARED A MOUSE
DECLARETH THAT
HE WOULD BECOME
A CAT. IF HE MIGHT
HAVE HIS DESIRE

If I might alter kind,
   what think you I would be?
Nor fish, nor fowl, nor flea, nor frog,
   nor squirrel on the tree.
The fish the hook, the fowl

A catty remark often has more lives than a cat.
Anon.

the limed twig doth catch;
The flea the finger, and the frog
  the buzzard doth dispatch.
The squirrel thinking naught,
  that featly cracks the nut,
The greedy goshawk wanting prey
 in dread of death doth put.
But scorning all these kinds,
  I woud become a cat,
To combat with the creeping mouse
  and scratch the screeking rat.
I would be present aye,
  and at my lady's call,
To guard her from the fearful mouse
  in parlour and in hall.
In kitchen for his life
  he should not show his head;
The pear in poke should lie untouched
  when she were gone to bed.
The mouse should stand in fear,
  so should the squeaking rat:
All this would I do if I were
  converted to a cat.

George Turberville

THE NIGHT IS A BIG BLACK CAT

The Night is a big black cat
  The Moon is her topaz eye,
The stars are the mice she hunts at night,
  In the field of the sultry sky.

G. Orr Clark

All cats are possessed of a proud spirit and the surest way to forfeit the esteem of a cat is to treat him as an inferior being.

Michael Joseph

Are cats lazy? Well, more power to them if they are. Which one of us has not entertained the dream of doing just as he likes, when and how he likes, and as much as he likes?

Fernand Mery

A kitten is more amusing than half the people one is obliged to live with.
Lady Sydney Morgan

Stretched pensively in noble attitudes,
Like sphinxes dreaming in their solitudes,
He seems to ponder in an endless trance;
With magic sparks his fecund loins are filled,
And, like fine sand, bright golden atoms gild
With vague and starry rays his mystic glance.

Baudelaire
from *Fleurs du Mal*

I can rarely remember having passed a cat in the street without stopping to speak to it.

Bruce Marshall

A cat can be trusted to purr when she is pleased, which is more that can be said for human beings.

William Ralph Inge

The cat is never vulgar.
Carl Van Vechten